RULE FOR A NEW BROTHER

RULE FOR A NEW BROTHER

Darton, Longman & Todd

London

First published in Great Britain in 1973 by
Darton, Longman & Todd Limited
85 Gloucester Road, London SW7 4SU
© 1973 Benedictine Priory 'Regina Pacis'
Printed in Great Britain by The Anchor Press Ltd
and bound by Wm. Brendon & Son Ltd
both of Tiptree Essex.

ISBN 0 232 51220 5

Regel voor een nieuwe broeder
by the Brakkenstein Community of
Blessed Sacrament Fathers, Holland

English translation by the
Benedictine Nuns of Cockfosters

Reprinted 1974 and 1975

The translators thank Fr. James Dekker, s.s.s., for his kindness
in putting his own translation of the original at their disposal;
Mrs. Rosemary Haughton and Dom Barnabas Sandeman, o.s.b.,
for their advice on style; and the author, Fr. Dr. H. van der Looy
of Brakkenstein, for his generous help and patience with the
translation.

Contents

1 *Seeking God*

Brother,
you want to seek God with all your life,
and love Him with all your heart.

But you would be wrong
if you thought you could reach Him.
Your arms are too short, your eyes are too dim,
your heart and understanding too small.

To seek God
means first of all
to let yourself be found by Him.
He is the God of Abraham, Isaac and Jacob.
He is the God of Jesus Christ.
He is your God,
not because He is yours
but because you are His.

To choose God
is to realise that you are known and loved
in a way surpassing anything men can imagine,

loved before anyone had thought of you
or spoken your name.

To choose God
means giving yourself up to Him in faith.
Let your life be built on this faith
as on an invisible foundation.
Let yourself be carried by this faith
like a child in its mother's womb.

And so,
don't talk too much about God
but live
in the certainty that He has written your name
on the palm of His hand.
Live your human task
in the liberating certainty
that nothing in the world can separate you
from God's love for you.

In Jesus of Nazareth
God shows in a special way
how urgently He seeks for man,
and how entirely He has committed Himself
to man's happiness.

In Jesus of Nazareth
a man shows
how completely we can belong to God;
how much freedom and humanity,
how much courage and self-forgetfulness
a man can possess
when he has been found by God
and has surrendered himself to Him.
In Jesus there is also a future for you
as you go by His road through sin and death
towards fellowship and love,
unfailing glory and life.

In faith you will recognise Him
in the works of His hands,
and above all in men,
men made in His image and likeness,
and most clearly of all in the love
which is Jesus.

But even if you receive no sign, no word from Him,
you will still recognise Him.
His very absence
is full of the mystery of his greatness.

It can help you
not to seek and serve some image of Him
you yourself have created.

So never let yourself lose heart
but go on seeking Him
in everything, in everybody—
they are all pledges
that you will finally meet Him.
Work hard to know Him
face to face.
For as sure as the dawn is His coming,
certain as the latter rains.

If you abide in love
you will abide in God
and not wander anymore in darkness.

Then live in joyfulness and hope,
unanxious, without any trace of fear,
at peace with yourself and the world,
in ceaseless reverence and thanks.
Because God's love for you endures for ever.

2 Following Jesus

Following Jesus
does not mean slavishly copying His life.
It means making His choice of life your own
starting from your own potential
and in the place where you find yourself.
It means living for the values
for which Jesus lived
and died.

It means following the path He took
and seeing things as He saw them.

If there is anything in which this life,
this way, can be expressed,
in which God has revealed Himself most clearly,
it is the reality of love.
You are someone
only in as far as you are love,

and only what has turned to love in your life
will be preserved.

What love is
you can learn from Jesus.

He is the one who has loved most.
He will teach you to put the centre of yourself
outside.
For no man has greater love
than he who lays down his life
for his friends.
He will also teach you
to be unlimited space for others,
invitation and openness:
'Come to me,
all who are weary and over-burdened
and I will give you rest.'

So be converted to love every day.
Change all your energies,
all your potential,
into selfless gifts for the other person.

Then you yourself will be changed from within
and through you
God's Kingdom will break into the world.

You are called to follow Jesus closely.
With Him you will take the road
up to Jerusalem,
the city of suffering and glorification.
With Him you will give everything
that the Kingdom may come.

On this road you are called
to be least of all and not master,
to carry other men's burdens
and not lay your own on them,
to give freedom instead of taking it,
to grow poor in order to make others rich,
to take the cross upon yourself
thus bringing joy to other men,
to die in order that others may live.
This is the mystery of the gospel
and there is no purpose in endless talk about it.
Be silent—for it will be true and genuine
only if you practise it.

So keep Jesus Christ before your eyes.
Don't hesitate to go anywhere He leads you;
don't stay where you are and don't look back,
but look forward with eagerness to what lies
    ahead.

3 *Members of One Body*

The community is the first place
where you will make God's kingdom incarnate.
It is one of the countless points
where God's new people assemble in peace,
in reconciliation, justice and joy,
in praise of God and service to the world.
A people whose King is the Lord.

Accept with gratitude
the brothers God gives you
to go with you on the way.
Your task is to serve and upbuild one another
as members of one body.

To the extent
that you are filled with His Spirit
and ready to die that others may live,
to that extent will you grow in unity
and reflect the face of Christ
more and more clearly.

And to the extent that you are ready
to die together
that others may live
will your community bear fruit
for the coming of the Kingdom.

Then put aside all ambition,
and no longer concentrate on yourself.
Be constantly converted to your brothers
and place yourself in God's hands.

Give instead of demanding,
trust others instead of compelling their trust,
serve instead of being served,
bless instead of cursing.
And be sure that when you have done all things
    well
you will still be an unprofitable servant.

So be attentive to the others,
not in order to dominate or exploit them
but to work for their happiness
discreetly and effectively
and to build them up
in all the riches of faith and love.

And you, accept from your brother
the help you need.

Be thankful for the variety of gifts
and difference of personality.
When you put your own potential
and insights at the service of your brothers
your unity will grow stronger and richer,
and together you will create that spaciousness
which finds room for everyone.

Pluriformity is not the end
but the means to make unity more powerful
and the individual bear more fruit.

Never be satisfied with what is imperfect
yet also realise
God is patient with us.
Let progress and development
be of such a sort that all can keep pace,
and never refuse to set out together
when in obedience to the gospel
the community travels on to a new future.

Make the effort
of listening to the other man
and of understanding him.
Give your opinion when it is useful
without false humility
or assertiveness.
Speak in such a way
that you can still hear what the other is saying,
and that he will still be ready to hear you.
Whether you speak or keep silent
let it proceed from the peace of the Lord.

Take no vengeance, not even in thought.
Avoid every tendency to depression and sadness—
it is death to your soul.
Look for the light in all things and all people.
Your night will be made radiant
by numberless stars
till the moment when the Sun of Justice
rises in your heart,
and that morning begins which knows no ending.

Your faith and love
must be constantly renewed;

your weakness and faults
constantly corrected.
Don't be afraid to open yourself to your brothers.
Choose from among them a sure and skilful guide
who will help you advance in the way of the Lord.

Never disappoint the trust
another man puts in you.
Be warm and merciful
and let none go from you empty-handed.
The least you can offer
is your time and patience,
your affection and your prayer.

The quality of your community
does not depend on age or numbers.
The only thing that counts
and will bring you a blessing
is that you should be always seeking each other
in the Spirit of Jesus.
From Him alone comes salvation.

Have great respect
for the seniors in the community.

Don't distress them
by your talk or behaviour.
Be gentle towards their weakness
and incapacities—
you are building on what they began.

Every body must have a head,
every circle a centre.
Joyfully, then, accept the man
who fulfils this special service.
More than anyone else
he needs your support and mercy.
Let him be for you as a presence of the Lord,
not because of his human qualities
and leadership,
but for the sake of his special calling
and grace.

Everything in your life
can have love as its motive, its end.
The vows by which you bind yourself
are precisely your own way
of embodying your love for God and man.

The more you grow in love,
the more clearly you will understand
what the vows demand;
and the more seriously you live your vows,
the more you will grow in love.

4 *For the Sake of the Kingdom*

Your vow to remain unmarried
for the sake of God's Kingdom
will draw you into the loneliness
of the cross of Jesus
and reveal the basic loneliness
of every man.
At the same time it invites you
to build up a fellowship with Him
and to establish the kingdom of love
among men.

By not marrying you put an end
to the cycle of procreation and death.
You are beginning a new kind of existence
in the incorruptibility
of a new-born generation,
and the unimagined fruitfulness of the Kingdom
    of God.

To be unmarried
does not mean for you the renouncing of love,
contempt for the body
or fear of marriage.
No,— it is the bringing of your potential for love
into the new and unlimited fruitfulness
of the Kingdom.

So you are called
to be a witness to love,
and its begetter,
an encouragement to all who are seeking
love's genuine image.

So you will also be a protest
against the narrow view
which identifies love with sex.

You will be able to do this
only if your deepest self is anchored in God,
as Jesus Himself bore witness:
I and the Father are one.
In Him you will find a love
which surpasses all human imaginings.

You will also have to be
a community man.
Make sure you don't grow isolated
from your brothers on the human level.
Open yourself to the joys
of life together as brothers;
foster a mature development of your feelings,
and a human warmth in your life.

Always be the first to love
and be faithful to that love
even if you get no answer.
Don't make conditions.
Be thankful and praise God
when you realise you are loved.

5 Called to Freedom

Following Jesus
demands of you in the first place
obedience to His Gospel.

You must place yourself,
alone and in community,
under the scrutiny of this Word,
and always be determining your conduct by it.
Then you will find the truth
to free you most radically,
and a solidarity
to make your community
a living gift to others.

Obedience also demands of you
that you listen to the other person;
not only to what he is saying
but to what he is.

Then you will begin to live in such a way
that you neither crush nor dominate
nor entangle your brother
but help him to be himself
and lead him to freedom.

Christ was thus obedient
unto death
so that we might be free men.
He was the least among the dead
that we might have life.

Don't be afraid then
that your obedience to the Gospel,
your listening to others,
will impoverish your personality
or decrease your responsibility.
It summons you rather
to live out your responsibility
in your encounter with others.

Never make the mistake of thinking
you can gain your freedom by your own exertions.
It is something which you give to others
and which you receive yourself from them.

No laws, no rules,
no therapy, no discussions are capable
of setting our communities in order
and making them fruitful
if the Spirit of Jesus is not master there.

In the community there will be someone
who exercises the service of authority.
His first task is to foster unity among you
and make the community grow
in faithfulness to its vocation.
His authority builds up the community,
but at the same time he has authority
only in so far as you are ready to obey him.

For the full development of each one's poten-
    tialities
a flexible yet definite structure is needed
to maintain the space
for living together.
You can't have a body without a skeleton,
or a river without banks to guide its stream.
Keep wholeheartedly to the arrangements that
    have been agreed:

then people will never rely on you in vain
and you will be able to put all your trust in others.

In obedience to each other and to the Gospel
you will discover the interior freedom
that makes you capable
of comprehending the world's needs—
without identifying in a shallow way
with special groups and causes—
and of entering into them yourself.

Man's freedom is being threatened more than ever.
Set yourself against everything that oppresses man.
Free yourself from a world
that seeks only pleasures and possessions
and bring others to share your freedom.
Set yourself against everything that makes men
    slaves
politically, economically, socially.
You have nothing to lose.

No doubt you will have noticed
that man's fundamental bondage
is to sin,
to his short-sighted attachment to himself.

Through your radical surrender to God
you will be freed from this
and become a deliverer of other men,
a breath of fresh air for those you meet,
a servant of all,
a source of life, expectation and hope.

6 *That we Might be Rich*

You are ready to put all you have
at the service of others.
You seek poverty not for its own sake,
nor from contempt or fear
for the good things God gives you,
but because you want to contribute something
to alleviate the world's poverty,
to make even your own possessions available.

Remember the words of Paul:
'You know the grace of our Lord Jesus Christ,
that though he was rich,
yet for your sake he became poor,
so that by his poverty you might become rich.'

The community is the place
where you daily share
riches and poverty,
energy and weakness,

joy and sorrow,
success and failure,
your hope and your doubt.
In this kind of community can grow
something of Christ's bond with His Father:
'All that I have is yours,
all that you have is mine.'

Live like a poor man
without parading your poverty.
Stand by the poor wherever they live and work.
Your first love must go out
to the least of men.
Don't tie yourself down to the rich or powerful
of the world.
Get rid of the inclination
to court the great and influential.
Otherwise you would deform
the image of the Church.

Put your trust in God,
wait for His mercy
and for all that you need.
Above all, take Jesus as your riches,

the pearl for which you will give everything,
your treasure in heaven.

Don't be romantic about this;
take your part in the simple struggle for a living,
but without attaching your heart
to what you earn by it.
In this way you will be able to help many people
and at the same time be a condemnation
of every form of materialism or snobbery.

Don't suppose poverty
consists only in big things.
Keep clear of all competitiveness and envy;
treat with care the things we possess in com-
    mon.
Be sober and restrained,
and don't wait till you are asked outright
before giving anything.
But don't suppose poverty
consists only in little things.
Share with the whole world.
A generous contribution to relieve poverty
is better than a little gift;

and an intelligent and effective effort
to fight the causes of poverty
is better than almsgiving.

Keep in mind also
how much you lack yourself;
be aware of your own poverty
and dare to hold out your hands
to receive from others
and to learn from them.

7 *The Breaking of the Bread*

By the grace of God
you have been called to a life
in which everything is inspired
by the sacrament of the Eucharist.
You must grow in daily knowledge
of this mystery,
and in a greater love for the Lord
who gives Himself in it.

The celebration of the Eucharist
is the centre of your life.
It is the highest expression
and the strongest support
of your life in community.
It is the beginning and end of your actions;
the source and consummation
of your service to God.

When you celebrate the memorial of Christ
give thanks to God
for His countless benefits.
Never tire of praising Him
one in heart and voice with your brothers,
and united with Christ, the sacrifice of praise.
Renew yourself in the spirit of love and unity
because you are sharing with your brothers
the same bread, the same cup.

The celebration of the Eucharist
would be nothing but a romantic or aesthetic
    sensation
should you forget
that the heart of it
is the self-giving of Jesus.
The sacrifice of yourself for the sake of the others
is the single foundation of every community.
Unite yourself with the Lord, then,
in a fruitful and acceptable offering
for the life of the world.

Each day you are nourished at the Lord's table
and filled with His riches.

So be ready to break
the bread of your life
for the poor and hungry everywhere in the world.
Keep nothing for yourself
but share with the others
all you have received from God's tenderness.

In the bread of the Eucharist
and the cup of blessing
Christ's presence is revealed
at its most intense.
Let your life be permeated
with a tremendous reverence
towards this mystery of faith.
Your adoration needs no justification
more than your love and wonder
for the infinite, delicate grandeur of God,
the unfathomable depths of Christ's gift.
Let His praise not depart from your lips.

Life drawn from the Eucharist
makes all kinds of demands on you
to proclaim the meaning and greatness of this
    mystery.

You are called especially
to give the sacrament its full effect
in unity, brotherhood and service.
The unity of all Christians
and all men
must be closest to your heart.
Always and everywhere you are called
to rise above oppositions and divisions
in the universal love of Christ.
Always look for what unites
and fight everything that estranges and
    separates
men from each other.

Your calling gives you the privilege
of living the eucharistic mystery to the full.
So reject nothing which the Church
enjoins on your faith,
and accept nothing that might obscure
the full meaning of this sacrament.

To Christ the Lord
who dwells ever present in His gifts
you can bring your life's adoration.

Your whole life must be worship
in spirit and truth,
your whole existence a celebration
and adoration of the presence of God.
Your life is to be poured out
in prayer and adoration
before the Eucharist,
and there it will be inspired afresh.
In this way give glory to the Father
through Him, in Him and with Him.

The Eucharist sets you on the way of Christ.
It takes you into his redeeming death
and gives you a share
in the most radical deliverance possible.
And already the light of the resurrection,
the new creation,
is streaming through it from beyond.
Whenever you sit at table with the risen Lord,
it is the first day of the week,
very early in the morning.

8 *Prayer*

The Lord Jesus Himself will teach you
how you should pray.
He is the creative Word
which you may receive in the silence of your
  heart
and the fruitful soil of your life.
Listen attentively to what He will say;
be swift to carry out
what He will ask of your.
You have been promised His Spirit
who will bear your poor little efforts
before the throne of grace
and into the intimacy of the living God.

Your prayer is therefore not so much a duty
as a privilege;
a gift rather than a problem
or the result of your own efforts.

So don't tire yourself out
looking for beautiful thoughts or words,
but stay attentive before God
in humility and expectation,
in desire and purity of heart,
full of joy and hope.
Your prayer will take countless forms
because it is the echo of your life,
and a reflection of the inexhaustible light
in which God dwells.

Sometimes you will taste and see how good the
    Lord is.
Be glad then, and give Him all honour,
because His goodness to you has no measure.
Sometimes you will be dry and joyless
like parched land or an empty well.
But your thirst and helplessness
will be your best prayer
if you accept them with patience
and embrace them lovingly.

Sometimes your prayer will be an experience
of the infinite distance that separates you from God;

sometimes your being and His fullness
will flow into each other.

Sometimes you will be able to pray
only with your body and hands and eyes;
sometimes your prayer will move beyond words
   and images;
sometimes you will be able to leave everything
   behind you
to concentrate on God and His Word.
Sometimes you will be able to do nothing else
but take your whole life and everything in you
and bring them before God.
Every hour has its own possibilities
of genuine prayer.

Don't be afraid to set apart
a considerable time for your prayer every day.
It is your vocation.
Your zeal for the Kingdom of God
and your availibility for all your brothers
will grow all the greater for it.
Remember that prayer is more powerful
than anything you can achieve by your actions.

And the Lord says there are evils
that can only be cast out
by prayer and fasting.

So set yourself again and again
on the way of prayer.
Never wait till you feel the need for it.
Often enough, if you only make a new start,
God will bring it to a good end.
Make use of a method when you need it.
Learn from your brothers
and study how the saints of God have prayed.

As you pray in community
you will discover the wide horizon of each
    prayer.
Rejoice to meet your brothers
in the presence of the Lord,
and to look with them to the Father of all light.
Let yourself be carried by the rhythm of prayer
in the peace and joy of a new world.
Let yourself be healed of the wounds
you suffer every day
by the saving praise of God.

Let yourself be renewed
in your faith, hope and love
by the Word that comes to you.
Don't let yourself be distracted by accidentals.
Try to understand God's Word
even in the mouth of a bad reader.
Don't be irritated
by the brother who sings off-key.
The forms are only important to the extent
that you know how to see through them.

Don't pray so that the world may admire you,
nor to draw men's eyes.
Pray so that God may be glorified
and His name praised.
Unite yourself with the unceasing prayer
of the Church on earth and in heaven.
Know that through your mouth and heart
all of creation is proclaiming the glory of God
and groaning for its redemption in the Lord.

In this way your life will be fed with prayer
and full of this search for God.
You will be able to give without counting the cost,

and accomplish God's will every day.
You will dedicate yourself heart and soul
to the battle against the powers of evil
and you will work
with joy and indestructible hope
for the new humanity
for which Jesus gave His life and blood.
Prayer and work
are not whole without each other.

9 *The Harvest is Great*

Your first task
is to co-operate in the building
of a brotherly community.
This is the condition and effect
of what we celebrate in the Eucharist.
In your community
begins the reality of the new humanity
in which the complex fragmentation
of our human existence and society of life
is healed and sanctified.

Your community does not exist for itself.
If it is truly evangelical
it will guide you and free you
to serve the people of God.
It is itself an active element
in realising the Kingdom.

God will urge you to go out from the community
to give form to His message of reconciliation
and unity among men.
Through the suffering and joy
of all whom you will encounter
you will let all your daily experience
reverberate through your prayer,
alone and with your brothers.

You have been called to be in the world
without being of the world.
If the salt loses its savour
it is good for nothing.
Therefore don't reject the world
and don't cut yourself off from people,
but love them as Jesus, the Redeemer, did.

But where the world
is nothing but the pride of life,
lust of the eyes, and desire of the flesh,
then flight alone is proper.
If you were to value this world
you could not be God's friend.

Your only ambition must be
to proclaim in word and deed
Christ's gospel of freedom,
justice and love.
For this use the most effective means
without supposing that they can replace God's grace.

You are free to do the work you want to do.
You can live as a religious and be a witness to the
    Lord
in every kind of work.
Discover for yourself
what seems the most fruitful field for you.
Be enterprising and creative.
God blesses the risks
undertaken for His sake.

When you choose your work be influenced
by its consequences for your life in community
and by the needs of the local church.
Preferably look for work
that you can do to the greatest benefit of the
    community
and in which it can support you most effectively.

Therefore always consult others.
You will thus prevent unnecessary conflicts
and avoid seeking yourself
or losing sight of your goal.

You are never alone in your work.
You can profit by the insights,
knowledge, experience and contacts of your
    brothers.
Be involved yourself with the whole group
and take interest in the work of others;
offer them your help where you can.

The love of Christ will not let you rest.
Your work is no escape into activity,
but a sharing in the upbuilding
of the body of Christ.
You can do this only on the basis
of an intimate union with Him
in purity of heart and selflessness.

It is not necessary to do your work
within a tight schedule
or the structure of a labour contract.

The community gives you the precious possibility
of committing yourself freely,
and developing your own initiatives
for the good of God's Kingdom.

If you think you are called
to the diaconate or priesthood
you are striving for something good.
See it as a high election,
a responsible mission.
It will be your task
to lead and instruct your people in the name of
    the Lord,
to sanctify and upbuild them in the Spirit.
This demands an obedient union with the bishop
and a collegial union with the other priests.

If you are called to the diaconate or priesthood,
it will mean a new call to holiness
and love for the Lord and His people.

10 *The Body of the Lord*

The way of Jesus
leads to communion with all people.
His enduring presence in the Church
is the foundation of a profound brotherhood
in the world
just as God desires it.

Love the Church as the Lord Himself.
Though she is burdened with the weakness
and sinfulness of a long history
she is still the instrument of His Kingdom,
His work of salvation for the world,
the germ of a new creation.

Show solidarity with all your brothers
and sisters in the faith.
One baptism and the same Eucharist
are the visible signs of your unity.

Be specially mindful of those
who are being persecuted by the world
for the sake of faith and righteousness.

Your love for the Church will also be expressed
in a union of faith with the Holy Father.
He fulfils a mission of unifying
and upbuilding for the whole Church.
Every fracture in the body
means a mutual impoverishment,
and conflicts with the will of the Lord.

If you love the Church
have a profound respect for her institutions and
    mission.
Whatever is impure and useless in her
must be healed, not attacked,
and purified in suffering rather than criticised.

Give yourself time to discover this Church
as a marvellously deep mystery
of fellowship in faith, hope and love,
transcending all barriers of time and space.
Built upon the foundation of the apostles and
    prophets,

she makes you members of the household
of all God's saints.

The Church comes into being
in the community where you live,
not so much in her official structures
as in her essential form of brotherhood
and new creation.

Remember then that your community
must before all else be one and holy,
catholic and apostolic.
In this way you will live the mystery of the
 Church
in the place where you are.

11 *The Spiritual Life*

Spiritual life
is life drawn from the Holy Spirit,
who raised Jesus from the dead
and turns the whole world into a new creation.

The Spirit within you
will bear fruit
of simplicity and goodness,
modesty and joy,
sobriety and gentleness.
He will give you interior freedom
and bring your love to perfection.
He will make you into a new man.

So don't carry on a futile battle against your-
    self,
don't divide yourself into good and evil.
Resist the temptation to analyse yourself—
turn your attention to the Lord instead,

and be deeply receptive.
Accept yourself in His light
and concentrate on the mission
you have to accomplish.

God's Spirit will bring you to simplicity
in an undivided dedication
to Him and to your fellowmen.
He gives you no programme
but the chance of turning yourself towards love
hour by hour.
And so spiritual life is not a burden
but a liberating vocation.
It is much more a matter of simplifying
than of complicated methods
and extraordinary performances.

In special cases it can be good
to impose some specific discipline on yourself.
Your daily life among your brethren and others
in service, openness and fidelity
is the usual form of ascesis,
which is both effective and enough.

Every day look at the way you are living
in the light of God's Word.
Let it warm you when you are cold,
encourage you when you are disappointed.
You must not only be a hearer of the Word—
you must also bring it to fulfilment.
Happy are you if you meditate upon it
daily in your heart:
you will be like a tree by the running water,
whose branches will stay fresh and green,
and they will keep bringing forth new fruit.

Spiritual life will develop
only in a climate of silence.
Bring the warring voices within you to still-
   ness.
Create an atmosphere of tranquillity and silence
with your brothers,
and so help each other to remain
concentrated on the presence of God.
It is also a sign of respect
for your brothers who are studying,
praying or resting.

You will surely have realised
that you cannot become a spiritual person
without an interior discipline
in your dealings with the world.
Don't let yourself be trapped into the unrest
that comes from excessive talking and gossiping.

Be discerning in your choice
of what the television, radio and papers offer-
    you.
Without a personal control
on your imagination and emotions
you will undermine your spiritual strength
and lessen your chances
of genuinely meeting and loving one another.

You will find a source of wisdom
and spiritual joy in the feasts of the Church.
The year is crowned with the signs
of God's goodness.
If you celebrate these feasts with the Church
then your own life and suffering,
your enthusiasm and work,

your dying and rising
and your waiting for the Lord
will receive significance and impact.

Never be misled by the thought
that after failing and sinning
there can be no forgiveness.
Look critically at your own shortcomings,
but be sure that with the Lord
there is always abundance of redemption.

Your spiritual life must be mobile;
travel from oasis to oasis.
Yet the Lord can prepare a table
even in the desert,
and in the furnace of trial
He will be coolness and refreshment.

12 *Mary*

Mary will have her own place in your life.
You cannot separate her from the Lord
who chose her as His mother and His bride.

She is the selfless space
where God became man;
she is the silence in which God's Word
can be heard.
She is the free woman, subject to none,
not even to the powers of evil.

She is the image of the Church.
Her self-effacing service will guide you to the
    Lord.
Her faith and fidelity
are a model for your life.

She has trodden all the paths
of our human existence;

she has gone through darkness and suffering,
through the abyss of loneliness and pain.

She is the little creature
through whom God's grandeur shines out;
she is the poor one
filled with divine riches.
She is wholly grace,
and grace for you.

Then take your part joyfully
in the prophecy of scripture:
'Behold, henceforth all generations
will call me blessed.'

13 *Off* Days and Years

Your life unfolds
in a continuous succession
of experiences and expectations.
No two days are the same,
no year leaves you unaltered.

Every day has enough trouble of its own.
When you go to sleep,
bury all that has happened in the mercy of God.
It will be safe there.
Stand back from what has happened,
and be grateful for it all.

When the day begins
be sure that you yourself can be
as new and pure as the new light.
It is like a resurrection.
The first hour is the most important of the day.
Don't yield to laziness,

but greet with joy
the new opportunities God offers you.

Even in the complicated world of today
try to keep close to a natural rhythm of life.
Meals taken together
should be moments of rest in your day.
See your encounters with others
as high peaks in your life,
and upbuilding.

The evenings are particularly suited
for talking and companionship,
joy and relaxation.
But here too the more you give
the more you will receive.
Be careful
not to prolong your evenings indefinitely.
In the long run it will produce nothing good.
If you are visiting friends,
don't keep them away from their rest
but know how to end your visit at a decent hour.

Your way through life
will not remain the same.

There are years of happiness and years of suffering.
There are years of abundance,
and years of poverty,
years of hope, and of disappointment,
of building up, and of breaking down.
But God has a firm hold on you through
    everything.

There are years of strength
and years of weakness,
years of certainty, years of doubt.
It is all part of life,
and it is worth the effort
to live it to the end
and not give up before it is accomplished.

You need never stop growing.
A new future is always possible.
Even on the other side of death
a new existence waits for you
in the fulness of that glory
which God has prepared for you
from the beginning.

14 *The End and the Beginning*

This rule is not meant to be a burden for you.
Nor does it pretend to be complete.
It should help you discover and experience
how great is the freedom to which you are
    called,
and how great the responsibility
which you may take upon yourself.
Be so faithful to this rule today
that you can be faithful again tomorrow.

Set out on the road together with your brothers,
together with the numberless people of God,
all pilgrims travelling to the Father's house.
Go on your way singing,
a song of hope on your lips
and your heart burning within you.
Now we have the alleluias of the journey,
soon there will be the alleluias of consummation,
of the great sabbath with God.

Now you are being sown
in the darkness of the earth;
when that day comes, you will bloom
in the light and warmth of God's eternity.

Set out on the road,
brother,
and peace be with you
for ever.